MW00884516

The Enoch Treasure

When God Walks With A Friend

To Sam'
Walk with God

The Enoch Treasure
When God Walks With A Friend

Christopher Cunningham, Ph.D.

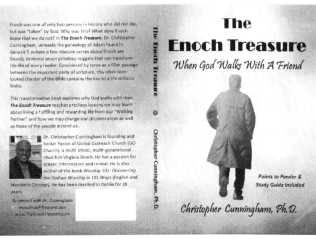

The Enoch Treasure

Christopher Cunningham, Ph.D.

The
Enoch Treasure

When God Walks With A Friend

Enoch was one of only two persons in history who did not die, but was "taken" by God. Why was this? What does Enoch know that we do not? In *The Enoch Treasure*, Dr. Christopher Cunningham, unmasks the genealogy of Adam found in Genesis 5 (where a few obscure verses about Enoch are found), to reveal seven priceless nuggets that can transform the life of every reader. Considered by some as a filler passage between the important parts of scripture, this often overlooked chapter of the Bible contains the key to a life without limits.

This transformative book explores why God walks with man, *The Enoch Treasure* teaches precious lessons we may learn about living a fulfilling and rewarding life from our "Walking Partner" and how we may change our circumstances as well as those of the people around us.

Dr. Christopher Cunningham is founding and Senior Pastor of Global Outreach Church (GO Church), a multi ethnic, multi generational church in Virginia Beach. He has a passion for prayer, intercession and revival. He is also author of the book *Worship 101: Discovering the God we Worship in 101 Ways* (English and Mandarin Chinese). He has been married to Dahlia for 28 years.

To connect with Dr. Cunningham
www.EnochTreasure.com
www.TheEnochTreasure.com

*Points to Ponder &
Study Guide Included*

Christopher Cunningham, Ph.D.

Cover and interior artwork & design:
Christopher Cunningham

Cover photo of trench coat man used by permission:
www.immediateentourage.com

Edited by Dahlia Cunningham
& Claudette Altman

For information write:
Global Outreach Church
333 Edwin Drive,
Virginia Beach, VA 23462
www.GOChurchVA.com
757-966-0312

ISBN-13: 978-1519497697
ISBN-10: 1519497695

Printed in the United States of America.

DEDICATION

*To Dahlia, my wife who has made it easier to
walk with God for more than half my life.*

*How beautiful on the mountains are
the feet of her who brings good news;
who walks wisely, smiles sincerely, loves lavishly,
serves sacrificially, gives generously and
steps stylishly into the unknown with God.*

CONTENTS

Walking Team

This is a book about walking—when God walks with a friend. I wish to say a special thanks to the friends who God has sent to walk alongside me, especially as I wrote this book.

First, I thank my beloved wife and ministry partner, Dahlia for being there even when the walk was along the steep hilly terrain. We might have taken the long way, but we know we'll get there some day.

Thanks to my mother, Claudette Brown who bought my first walking shoes, and continues to cheer me along. To my sister-in-law Claudette Altman, thanks for being a constant encouragement on our walking team. Thanks also to my siblings and other relatives who gave me lots of great stories to tell along the way.

Finally, heartiest thanks to my GO Church family for letting me lead you and trying out my sermons on you. You make the walk well worth it.

PREFACE

Hello Beautiful People. The book you now hold in your hand is a book that was birthed as a surprise. It came to me at a time I wasn't looking for any deep truths from scripture – I was simply having my daily devotions, taking care of my regular "Christian disciplines."

As it happens in the life of many Christians, I was in a bit of a slump. You know how slumps can be – once you begin to slip, it can take a crazy long time for you to pull yourself out. Having been there before, I decided not to let it happen to me again that time, so I decided I would do the bare minimum – sometime in the morning, I would scan through two or three chapters of the Bible – no big deal, five to ten minutes tops.

Not feeling particularly inspired, I decided to simply read through the Bible, a few minutes per day, beginning in Genesis. I had read the Bible cover to cover on several occasions, perhaps four or five times. So I started and knocked off the first three chapters on day one. On the second day I picked it up at Genesis Chapter Four, thinking I would hit three or four quick chapters and then move on with my day, and then it happened!

Genesis Five – the Book of the Genealogy of Adam. Every now and then you stumble onto these apparently "filler passages" in the Bible that seem to have been put there as a transition between the important parts. Then somewhere in the middle of the passage I tripped over it – the *Enoch Treasure*. It was always there, hidden in plain sight, as if God was having fun with us – it seems as if God was saying to me, "I can put my deepest truths right in front of you, and I can choose to reveal them whenever I want to."

I tripped over it – the Enoch Treasure. It was always there, hidden in plain sight.

The truth about the *Enoch Treasure* is so simple, yet profound, that I was stuck in this particular chapter of the Bible for about six months… so much for my plan to breeze through the Bible. God is like that; sometimes, He ruins our ill-conceived plans.

This passage changed my life forever and it may change yours too. There is so much packed into the few verses about Enoch, it will take us perhaps a lifetime to live it out. I am still living out the truths of this passage. Soon after my camping at this passage, I had the opportunity to share what I had gleaned with my congregation and I must confess, I was a bit surprised by the positive reactions. People kept coming to me and talking about how they never would have thought there was so much in this passage that they had always just overlooked.

There is so much packed into the few verses about Enoch, it will take us perhaps a lifetime to live it out.

I put the message away for some three years, only drawing on bits of it from time to time. Finally, my wife, Dahlia had a family reunion at which I was asked to minister in a special service. I felt the *Enoch Treasure* would be particularly useful for the family, several members of whom were not Christians. I shared the message and then we had the concluding activities of the reunion and we were off. No one really said anything much about the message, except a couple who noted that they felt it was very relevant for the reunion.

However, more than a month later, we were having a discussion on a newly formed *WhatsApp* family forum created at the reunion, when someone remarked that I don't normally say much, unless I am preaching, at which time I have the ability to find a remote passage and make it into the most meaningful sermons.

Next, one of my wife's nephews chimed in and agreed – he mentioned that he hadn't been to church in a long time, and he doesn't even like the church, as he believes it is the reason for many of the wars the world has had, but he was really impressed by the message. Without any further prompting, he began to outline all I had said in the message – I was taken aback. Could it be that the *Enoch Treasure* is so simple it can be remembered by almost anyone?

A few months later, one of my best friends went home to be with the Lord. She had asked me before her death to speak at her Celebration of Life service. Being both a pastor and so close to this wonderful saint was challenging, as I was involved with both comforting the family, dealing with my own grief as well as taking care of the arrangements for the service.

I hardly even had time to think about what I would talk about in the service. However, having shared on the *Enoch Treasure* fairly recently, I felt it would be quite appropriate to speak on it at the service, as it holds many secrets about both how to live and how to die.

I spoke on the *Enoch Treasure* and after the service it was as if a veil had been lifted and God was showing me how important this message was that He had revealed to me so long ago. Many people wanted to know if I had recorded the message.

One person, who had been a Christian for more than 30 years, remarked that never in his life had he seen someone "take such a boring passage and made it so exciting." A week later, I was at a dinner event when a number of people who attended the celebration service came to me and kept talking about the *Enoch Treasure*. They noted that it was all they were hearing anyone who attended the service talk about.

The final confirmation that this book needed to be written came when a missionary friend whom I respect very much, emailed me asking if I would send her my notes from the "funeral sermon." She wanted to use it as an upcoming message. The Bible says:

> "By the mouth of two or three witnesses every word shall be established"
> (2 Corinthians 13:1).

God had confirmed His word to me more than three times. He was saying, I have given you this message, for this time – now it's time for you to unlock the secrets of the *Enoch Treasure* to the world.

So what exactly is the *Enoch Treasure*? That's why you are holding this book in your hands. God is about to reveal His heart to you about the relationship He wants to have with you. However, before revealing the nuggets to be found in Genesis 5, you must pass through one important initiation rite – I warn you, it may be a little tedious, but it is well worth it. What's that initiation rite?

Don't lose heart, don't skip through it, no cheating now: Read Genesis Chapter 5, in its entirety...word for word. By the time you finish reading this book, you will never see the passage the same way again, nor will you ever be able to see the Bible the same way.

Are you ready? Let's go.

Genesis 5 NKJV

The Family of Adam

This is the book of the genealogy of Adam. In the day that God created man, He made him in the likeness of God. [2]He created them male and female, and blessed them and called them Mankind in the day they were created. [3]And Adam lived one hundred and thirty years, and begot *a son* in his own likeness, after his image, and named him Seth. [4]After he begot Seth, the days of Adam were eight hundred years; and he had sons and daughters. [5]So all the days that Adam lived were nine hundred and thirty years; and he died.

[6]Seth lived one hundred and five years, and begot Enosh. [7]After he begot Enosh, Seth lived eight hundred and seven years, and had sons and daughters. [8]So all the days of Seth were nine hundred and twelve years; and he died.

[9]Enosh lived ninety years, and begot Cainan. [10]After he begot Cainan, Enosh lived eight hundred and fifteen years, and had sons and daughters. [11]So all the days of Enosh were nine hundred and five years; and he died.

[12]Cainan lived seventy years, and begot Mahalalel. [13]After he begot Mahalalel, Cainan lived eight hundred and forty years, and had sons and

daughters. [14]So all the days of Cainan were nine hundred and ten years; and he died.

[15]Mahalalel lived sixty-five years, and begot Jared. [16]After he begot Jared, Mahalalel lived eight hundred and thirty years, and had sons and daughters. [17]So all the days of Mahalalel were eight hundred and ninety-five years; and he died.

[18]Jared lived one hundred and sixty-two years, and begot Enoch. [19]After he begot Enoch, Jared lived eight hundred years, and had sons and daughters. [20]So all the days of Jared were nine hundred and sixty-two years; and he died.

[21]Enoch lived sixty-five years, and begot Methuselah. [22]After he begot Methuselah, Enoch walked with God three hundred years, and had sons and daughters. [23]So all the days of Enoch were three hundred and sixty-five years. [24]And Enoch walked with God; and he *was* not, for God took him.

[25]Methuselah lived one hundred and eighty-seven years, and begot Lamech. [26]After he begot Lamech, Methuselah lived seven hundred and eighty-two years, and had sons and daughters. [27]So all the days of Methuselah were nine hundred and sixty-nine years; and he died.

[28]Lamech lived one hundred and eighty-two years, and had a son. [29]And he called his name Noah, saying, "This *one* will comfort us concerning our work and the toil of our hands, because of the ground which the LORD has cursed." [30]After he begot Noah, Lamech lived five hundred and ninety -five years, and had sons and daughters. [31]So all the days of Lamech were seven hundred and seventy-seven years; and he died.

[32] And Noah was five hundred years old, and Noah begot Shem, Ham, and Japheth.

Nugget 1
MORE THAN LIVING

Because you are reading a book called *The Enoch Treasure*, no doubt the name Enoch jumped off the page at you as you read the passage. Did you notice the huge difference in the passage when it talked about Enoch, than when it talked about everyone else? This passage outlines the first ten generations of the genealogy of Adam. In each case, we read that each man lived a certain number of years, had descendants and then died.

However, when we get to Enoch, the passage suddenly changes and we read something new that has not been mentioned in the Bible before: "Enoch walked with God." This little word, *walked* is pivotal. It is sandwiched in the middle of the passage and is easy to miss, but we must not… because from this we get the first nugget of the *Enoch Treasure*:

*Living is different
from walking with God.*

Everyone else lived; but Enoch walked with God.

According to the medium fertility estimate by the United Nations Department of Economic and Social Affairs, Population Division, the world population is about 7.3 billion people (July 2015 estimate). That's a whole lot of people living. Of all the people living today, how many can it truly be said of that they are walking with God? If Moses was writing about your life right now, would he say you are living, or walking with God?

If Moses was writing about your life right now, would he say you are just living, or walking with God?

We will examine what it means to walk with God more a little later, but it is good to know that *if Enoch walked with God, then God was also walking with Enoch*. Why is it that God would choose to walk with His creation? Walking with God is a way of saying there was a mutual friendship relationship between Enoch and God. But why would God desire to have a friendship, walking together relationship? The answer may surprise you. In Genesis 1:27, we read:

> "So God created man in His *own* image; in the image of God He created him; male and female He created them."

Further in that same chapter we notice:

> "Then God saw everything that He had made, and indeed *it was* very good"
> (verse 31).

Notice, God created man in His own image, and then confirmed that His creation was very good. Just half a chapter later, in Genesis 2:18 we see that God himself said:

> "*It is* not good that man should be alone; I will make him a helper comparable to him."

We just saw that man was created "very good," yet after that God stepped back and said this perfect being should not be alone. So if God made man in His own image, and said that man in his perfect state should not be alone, it also follows that God in His perfect state is also a relationship being. He desires to have a relationship with us. He wants to be friends with us; He wants to walk with us.

All throughout history, we have seen that God has been looking for people He can walk with... people who will be His special friends. Therefore, the *Enoch Treasure* is primarily discovering riches in being a friend of God. God wants to be our friend. His eyes search throughout the earth to find people who will be His friends, and as we will see in the coming pages, whenever He finds a good friend, He does something very special for them.

> *God in His perfect state is also a relationship being. He desires to have a relationship with us.*

There are friends and there are friends. A person who has unreliable friends will soon come to ruin, but that is not how God is... He is a friend who sticks closer to us than a brother, a friend who will make sacrifices for His walking buddies.

DIFFERENT FRIENDSHIPS

Who is a friend? Friendship is sometimes defined as a close and caring relationship between two people that is mutually satisfying. It is more than someone who will put his or her arm around you. Friendships are much more than merely social relationships.

These days we have different types of friends. There is the best friend forever (BFF). Sometimes a person has one BFF and then they move away and find another BFF. There are friends you have not seen in years but meet again and it's as if you never left each other.

Then there is the Facebook friend. I have more than a thousand Facebook friends – do you think I know each of them? Are you kidding me? Sometimes I receive friend requests and I have to look at their pictures to see if I know them. If I don't, I look to see who their friends are, and the type of posts they make, and then I decide if I will accept their friend request. This is certainly not how we developed friendships a few years ago.

People sometimes discredit these online friendships, but two researchers – Walter and Parks argue that online friends develop relationships that are just as close as those that they develop face to face. They actually have an official and important sounding name for this – *social information processing theory.*

Regardless of the label we put on it, the friendship with God concept is a revolutionary concept in religions – the undeniable fact that God wants to be our friend. There are several religions that see God as Father: Christianity, Judaism, Mormonism, Bahai, Krishnaism, etc., all see Him as Father; the one who created everything.

Some religions go even further to see God as Friend – Christianity, Judaism, the Sunni sect of Islam see him somewhat as a friend, a more personal being, while Shia Muslims do not see him as personal. However, the idea of a God who sacrifices to make friendship work is revolution-ary. How can it be that God will make sacrifices to become a friend of people He created? That is unheard of in any other religion.

God breathed breath into man and man became a living being. God would regularly walk through the Garden of Eden with Adam and Eve (Genesis 3:8), the first two people created. However, once they sinned, God had to drive them out of the garden. No longer would He walk with them as He did before.

There is something important to note: Our sins do not change God; they change us. After they sinned, Adam and Eve no longer walked with God, but God was and still is a relationship being.

The idea of a God who sacrifices to make friendship work is revolutionary.

Since Adam, humans have had the DNA of the breath of God flowing through their bodies. However, it's not everyone who walks with God. This is something we have to choose to do – will we merely live, or will we walk with God?

Prayer

Father, I do not want to be like the majority of people in the world, who merely live. I want to be someone You will delight to walk with. I want to walk with You every day of my life. I want to be Your friend, but not just any friend; I want to have the sort of relationship with You that transforms every aspect of my life. I pray this in Jesus name, Amen.

Nugget 2
THE REGULAR LIFE

If you are like me, you probably are wondering what made Enoch so special – what was inside him that caused him to have the kind of relationship that he had with God. If he had a secret formula, I want to find it, so that I can copy it. If he had some special characteristics, I want to discover them. I want to also have the sort of relationship Enoch had with God. However, our second nugget from the passage shows that Enoch had no secret DNA that made him special.

> *It is possible to walk with God and live a regular life.*

In Genesis 5 we read that Enoch had sons and daughters. That means he was "doing the deed." Enoch was a married man who most likely lived with his wife, worked and provided for his family. We do not know what his occupation was, but based on the time he lived, he most likely would have been a farmer. Yes, Enoch was someone who got his hands dirty, yet kept his heart clean. His clothes may have been soiled and his body wet from a hard day's labor, but his spirit was pure and his soul cleansed.

Today we live in a world often driven by sex. Sex sells. Sex ruins the lives of presidents and paupers alike. It destroys families, ends careers and causes many rifts to be created between friends. But sex was not meant to be something bad. God created sex – He meant for it to be enjoyed within the confines of marriage. We have in many ways redefined sex – we do our own thing our own way and call good evil and evil good.

Enoch had sex, probably lots of it, producing sons and daughters – yet he walked with God. In other words he enjoyed the pleasures of life, while still handling his sexual life in a way that brought glory to God, his friend.

When we close our bedroom doors to enjoy intimate pleasures with our partner, God does not close His eyes in embarrassment. He does not sneak out of the room – His name is Jehovah - Shammah – the Lord is Present (Ezekiel 48:35). Yes, you can still live your life, "do the deed" and not be embarrassed before God, because sex is not dirty. "Marriage is honorable and the bed is undefiled" – when we do it God's way.

When Dahlia and I got married, we were glad that we had saved ourselves for that very special someone and we believed we would have a lifetime together of enjoying each other. Just as we did before any good meal (and even bad ones), on our wedding night, we committed our sexual lives to the Lord. In a way, you could say we "said grace" before eating.

Enoch enjoyed the pleasures of life, while still handling his sexual life in a way that brought glory to God

Too many people are embarrassed by sex. We don't have to be. Even if your life did not start out God's way, it is probably not too late for you to right the ship. You may not be walking with God in the area of sex, but He is the kind of friend who forgives and allows us to change.

Our sexual lives are very important, and Enoch shows that God does not have to be left out of this significant part of our lives. In fact, God ought not to be left out of any aspect of our lives.

You may be in the military and wonder if it is

possible to walk with God while holding a weapon in your hand. Is it possible to walk with God while being in the dug-out, is it possible to walk with Him, while having to make important life or death decisions? The answer is: Absolutely! You can walk with God while living an ordinary life.

It is possible to walk with God while being in the dug-out

Politicians and lawyers are often ridiculed in their professions. Can a politician walk with God and serve the people? The truth is, politicians, lawyers, judges, prison guards and inmates alike CAN walk with God, but more so, need to walk with HIM. Your jobs are too hard to try to go it any other way.

Teachers – don't walk into the classroom alone, walk with God there and your students will experience a touch from the master's hand as you teach. Business professionals, you have a job to do, connections to make, schedules to keep – but your best asset is not your skills in wealth building or marketing, your best asset is a relationship with the One who wants to walk with you.

Living a regular life and walking with God is

not just important as you go out into the world to earn a living. The young mother breastfeeding her infant child, the unemployed dad combing through the classifieds, the retiree on a budget, and even the dreamer obsessing over the "next big thing" without a way to bring it to pass – you are all candidates for walking with God.

Another important point to understand from the fact that Enoch lived a regular life, yet walked with God is that there are a whole lot more ordinary people than celebrities. Was Enoch popular? Perhaps not, while he was living, but he is today. **He is only one of two people who never tasted death** (the other being Elijah) – we'll come back to that later.

Enoch was not like Job, who had riches written about in the Bible. He did not slay his thousands like King David. He built no temple like Solomon, led no revivals like Josiah, and redeemed no people like Moses. If he were in a race, he probably would have been relegated to the status of "also ran." He was by no means a celebrity, he simply walked with God – but that earned him the best prize.

CELEBRITY WORLD

We live in a celebrity driven world. Singers, musicians, actors and even in the church we have celebrity ministers. I am not knocking this – many people have paid their dues and are now reaping the benefits of their hard work in the form of huge followings. I know of some celebrity ministers and bishops who I genuinely believe are walking with God – their lives reflect a true commitment to God.

Of course there have been those who have simply been fortunate to be in the right place at the right time, and have experienced the proverbial 15 minutes of fame. In fact, there are some socialites who are simply famous for being famous.

He was by no means a celebrity, he simply walked with God – but that earned him the best prize.

Then there are those who remain famous, long after they have passed from this life. Some 40 years after his death, Elvis Presley the king of rock-and-roll is still as popular in some circles as he ever was. He is still the highest selling individual artist of all time with more than 260 million certified units sold (claimed 600 million, per CNNmoney.com). There are hundreds of Elvis impersonators and people even build shrines to him in their homes.

Bob Marley, the king of reggae died at the age of 36, yet he still sells millions of records and is named as one of the world's best-selling artists of all time, with more than 36 million certified units sold (unofficial 75 million).

If Elvis were alive today (some say he is), he would be older than 80 and Bob Marley would be older than 70 years old – both most likely retired. However, these celebrities and many others will continue to live on through their music and art-work for decades to come. Only time will tell how much longer the fame of these celebrities will live on. But because he walked with God, Enoch never faced death – he lives on. This brings us to the third important nugget from our passage.

Prayer

Lord Jesus, I invite You into every aspect of my life. I commit my sexual life to You. I commit my appetites and all my desires to You. I want You to take all of me. I want to walk with You, not just in some areas, but I make You Lord over all of my life. Amen.

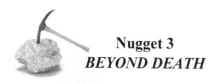

Nugget 3
BEYOND DEATH

Enoch did not die, the Lord took him; he was the first person raptured. Genesis 5:24, tells us "And Enoch walked with God; and he *was* not, for God took him." Notice that everyone else lived, had children… and then they died. However, with Enoch it was different, he was taken.

Some may look at the passage and argue that "and he was not, for God took him" does not necessarily mean he didn't die, it could be that one day he went into the mountains, died there and God took him, without anyone else finding him. The writer of Hebrews removes all such doubt.

Hebrews 11:5-6 tells us:

"By faith Enoch was taken away so that **he did not see death**, and was not found, because God had taken him; for before he was taken he had this testimony, that he pleased God."

God had a friendship relationship with Enoch, which was so good that God said: I cannot bear to be away from my friend anymore, I want him now. He was taken and did not see death. From this, we get the third nugget.

Being taken is different from dying.

So here is a formula of sorts: First – If being taken is different from dying, it means you can be taken without dying. If you can be taken to heaven without dying, then it follows that you can be taken and returned without dying. Whoa... did I really say you can go to heaven without dying? Yes, I did – and I am not talking about near death experiences.

I grew up in a church that was very Bible based. If you cannot back something up with scripture, then that's a theology you need to get rid of. Further, you are not to build a theology around one verse of scripture – scripture interprets scripture and scripture reinforces scripture. It is therefore important to see if the Bible teaches that we can go to heaven without dying.

A second person who had a similar experience to Enoch was the prophet Elijah. Elijah makes a grand entrance onto the pages of the Bible with a pronouncement to King Ahab that there will be a massive drought on the land except at his word. Those are bold statements coming from anyone – unless they can be backed up.

However, the Bible tells us that, "the people who know their God shall be strong, and carry out *great exploits*" (Daniel 11:32). And so, from his first appearance, Elijah was carrying out great exploits. Why, because of the close friendship he had with God.

You may read about Elijah's journey as he walked with God in the biblical narrative of 1&2 Kings. One thing you may find strange is that, though he walked with God, Elijah was a loner who saw little positive results to his ministry. It is so easy to see poor results as a sign that we are doing the wrong thing. That is not always the case.

Elijah lived in a period of spiritual apostasy where hardly anyone worshipped God, turning rather to the lifeless Baal, and other idolatrous worship. Yet, Elijah separated himself from the evil around him, choosing instead to walk with God.

The Bible does not tell us how Enoch was

"taken" by God, but we have an indication of the sort of special ceremony it may have been by how Elijah, the only other person who did not see death, was taken up to heaven.

As Elijah journeyed with his assistant, Elisha, it became known to him that his Master would be "taken" by God that day. "Then it happened, as they continued on and talked, that suddenly a chariot of fire *appeared* with horses of fire, and separated the two of them; and Elijah went up by a whirlwind into heaven" (2 Kings 2:11). Wow, only one other person witnessed it, yet God pulled out all the stops to welcome His friend home – without him tasting death.

Though he walked with God, Elijah was a loner who saw little positive results to his ministry.

VISITING HEAVEN

While Enoch and Elijah never experienced death, yet went to heaven, others have been to heaven before their death. Every one of the original apostles walked with Jesus from the beginning. After Jesus' ascension, Peter stood up in the midst of the disciples and asserted that in keeping with scripture, another should take the place of Judas, the betrayer, who had committed suicide. This replacement needed to be:

"of these men who have accompanied us all the time that the Lord Jesus went in and out among us, beginning from the baptism of John to that day when He was taken up from us" (Acts 1: 21-22).

As one who met the above criteria, Matthias was the one chosen to replace Judas. However, we hear very little about Matthias after this as God had other plans—He chose a man by the name of Saul.

After living a life in opposition to God, Saul had a dramatic conversion and was renamed Paul. Paul never met the Lord Jesus personally, while Jesus was alive, so he would have been disqualified to be an apostle, However, he met Jesus after Jesus had died, was buried, resurrected and gone back to heaven. Where did Paul meet Jesus? The Apostle Paul once had a heavenly experience that he found difficult to put into words. He writes about it in 2 Corinthians 12:2-5:

> I know a man in Christ who fourteen years ago – whether in the body I do not know, or whether out of the body I do not know, God knows – such a one was caught up to the third heaven. [3] And I know such a man – whether in the body or out of the body I do not know, God knows – [4] how he was caught up into Paradise and heard inexpressible words, which it is not lawful for a man to utter. [5] Of such a one I will boast; yet of myself I will not boast, except in my infirmities.

We cannot be dogmatic about what happened when Paul met Jesus, as even Paul is sketchy about this, but it is possible that Paul experienced a sort of one-on-one tutelage from Jesus that absolutely transformed his life. Paul became not just an apostle, but one of the foremost apostles, who wrote more than half of the New Testament.

Another person who had an experience while still alive was the apostle and prophet John. One Sunday, he was in the Spirit when he experienced a sort of out of body experience, which took him to heaven.

In Revelation 4, we read:

"After these things I looked, and behold, a door *standing* open in heaven. And the first voice, which I heard *was* like a trumpet speaking with me, saying, "Come up here, and I will show you things which must take place after this."

It is possible that Paul experienced a sort of one-on-one tutelage from Jesus that absolutely transformed his life

The book of Revelation came out of a heavenly experience John had. He was "taken" and walked around and saw the throne and worshippers, and angels, etc. The experience did not take John's life – that is why he was able to return from the experience to give us this important prophetic book, which is so relevant to us today. Did John physically go to heaven in the flesh, or was he merely seeing a vision? What difference does it make? He was there.

We can make a trip there as well, on the Holy Spirit Express. The Apostle Paul after having his own heavenly experiences writes to the church in Ephesus and tells them that through the finished work of Jesus on the cross, God has "raised *us* up together, and made *us* sit together in the heavenly *places* in Christ Jesus."

Many Christians have gotten to the stage where we are so satisfied with warm goose bump feelings in a Sunday morning service. If we sense God's presence in worship, that's the ultimate for us. We feel it is good enough, but God wants more for us. He loves us and wants to have a deep relationship with us and He will take us into heavenly places to be with Him.

There are Christians who have shared testimonies of having had "Throne Room experiences." I confess that so far I have not. Although, in the past I have had experiences in the middle of sleep, where the atmosphere in the entire room changes and I feel an energy surrounding me, and I feel myself being lifted, going up.

At first, it scared me ascending into the sky and passing stars and then looking down at stars. Did these experiences really happen in the physical or were these visions? Like Paul, I don't know, but I couldn't understand what was happening to me because I had no compass for this sort of thing – Up to that point, I had never heard that it happened to anyone else.

Much later, I heard others who had experienced the same thing and I have a couple of friends who have experienced the exact thing I described. One female friend described it as "falling up." Yep… sounds about right.

Not every Christian will experience this sort of phenomenon, but whether it happens in the physical or in a vision or not, it is still possible to have heavenly experiences in a spiritual sense. As we worship the Lord, we are seated in heavenly places with Him. As we look around heaven, we see things not as they are on earth. We see them as God sees them with new eyes.

We can make a trip to heaven as well, on the Holy Spirit Express

That then changes the way we pray because we no longer pray amiss – we declare things the way they are in heaven, for them to come to the earth.

We have the power to do this. We can bring them here…Just as I have seen the worship in heaven, I will not stop until the whole earth is filled with heavenly worship.

To the mother or father praying for a lost child: Go to heaven in the spiritual realm and see the child God sees, then declare, Lord, I want that child who I see in heaven. To the person praying for someone who is sick – there is no sickness in heaven. See the situation as God sees it in heaven.

That's why when we pray we say: "Thy kingdom come, thy will be done as it is in heaven." How do we know how it is in heaven? We look and see things in the heavenly realm where we see God. This is not just an Enoch thing.

Let us not be satisfied by feeling the presence of God in a service or having a "personal revival." Let us continue until we have had a personal encounter with the Most High. The Bible was not written to tell us fancy things about those days; if it was good in those days, it is good for us today.

Beautiful People, don't stop until you find God in the secret place and have a personal encounter with the Most High. It is time to get back to the secret place. That's what Enoch did. While he was working, taking care of his regular activities etc., enjoying a boisterous laugh that probably caused him to roll on the floor in delight, he found time to be in the secret place with God.

Here is a radical thought – Could we become such good friends of God that He will feel that He is denying Himself if He does not come to be with us?

As we look around heaven, we see things not as they are on earth. We see them as God sees them

Prayer

Dear God, I just want to be with You in the secret place because You are kind, You are good, You are wonderful, You are just, You are merciful. I just want to be with You. Better is one day in Your courts than a thousand elsewhere, so God, while I live, let me walk in the glory of Your presence, every day. I pray this in Jesus name, Amen.

Nugget 4
WALK AND LEARN

So far we have seen how living is different from walking with God; it is possible to walk with God and live a regular life and being taken is different from dying. These nuggets came directly from the passage, but our next nugget comes more from an understanding of the dynamics of "walking together" for an extended time, though as you will see, it continues to build on the foundation of the Genesis 5 passage.

> *When you walk with God, you know His ways.*

As we already saw, Enoch not only lived, but his relationship with God was similar to walking buddies. My wife recently formed a walking group of a few women. They walk at Mt. Trashmore Park, so named because it was once a landfill, but after years of mounting trash, the landfill was converted into a beautiful park, which now attracts hundreds of thousands of walkers and other visitors each year.

One lap around Mt. Trashmore, including the "mountain" and a large lake is approximately 5 kilometers. The team of women will walk around the park for approximately one hour each time. Sometimes different women will join the group, but there is a core of about five women who are almost always there. The purpose of the walks is exercise and so the women walk briskly.

However, over time, these women have gotten to know each other better as they walk together. This was an obvious side benefit of walking together, though the main purpose is health related.

Now think of a hypothetical scenario in which an elderly man, Jon is custodian for a large facility. Each day he goes through the facility taking care to clean the restrooms, sweep and mop the floors, and when everything is ready, he opens the doors, turns on the air conditioning, making sure the temperature is at the correct levels, preparing the restrooms, etc.

One day Jon gets an assistant, Luke. However, Jon does not do what most supervisors would do, which is to train Luke how to do the job properly, and then giving him responsibilities along the way. Instead, Jon is happy just to have Luke's company and so rather than becoming a real assistant, Luke becomes Jon's walking buddy as Jon does all the work. Day in, day out, the same thing happens over and over again.

One day, Jon wakes up and can hardly move – the years of tireless working with no breaks finally caught up with him. Jon calls in sick and asks Luke to take care of things for him. What is Luke's response? No problem, buddy, I have it covered. You get some rest and I will take care of things for you. Luke then goes about taking care of everything Jon would have done and he does not call Jon even once to ask him what to do.

Why? Because Luke walked with Jon and observed everything that Jon did. He didn't need to ask which detergent Jon used on the floor or where the mops were to be found. He knew the proper temperature at which each room should be set, and where to find the keys for each door.

Unlike other days, a new situation came up that Luke had never seen Jon deal with before – someone had spilled something on one of the walls and in trying to clean it off, the person stripped the paint off a small section of it. Luke immediately knew how to handle it – he went directly to the paint room, got the "touch up brush" and the matching paint and in a few minutes, the wall was looking as good as new.

Luke didn't have to see Jon do everything. He walked with him long enough to know exactly what Jon would have done in that situation.

It was no different for Enoch and God – as Enoch walked with God for 300 years, he learned God's ways. He knew the things God liked and didn't like. He knew what made God happy and when his life displeased Him – and yes, Enoch was not sinless, he made mistakes from time to time.

I imagine that sometimes Enoch said or did some things that he immediately knew displeased God. But Enoch knew God was holy and so he needed to keep short accounts with God, meaning he did not wait very long to make things right; he apologized quickly, and continued to walk with God.

DAILY WALK
Sometime ago, the phrase "What would Jesus do?" (WWJD), went viral. People wore wristbands

to remind themselves when faced with varying situations what Jesus would have done when faced with similar situations. Enoch saw what God had done for so long, he no longer had to ask, WWJD? He knew.

Enoch knew what made God happy and when his life displeased Him – and yes, Enoch was not sinless

Today, we have God's word, the Bible to guide us in our daily walk with God. The more we read God's word the more we learn His ways. That means we know what Jesus is doing in every situation…and if we don't know, we can make an educated guess about how He would treat each situation.

Jesus was never a first responder, but a first responder who has been walking with God, has an instinctive flow, that comes from a place of knowing what the Heavenly Father desires in different situations. So is it with any training in the military or security forces – you are trained for different situations, but the scenarios you meet on the battlefield or streets will differ each time – yet there need not be much hesitation about how to handle the unknown when you know the All-Knowing God.

A college degree trains a person how to acquire knowledge – it does not fill graduates with all the knowledge they will ever need. However, when a well-equipped graduate faces the work-world, there ought to be an ease that comes when presented with new problems, not because he or she has faced that problem before. Rather, it's because the student has walked with professors who have helped to equip them with problem-solving skills.

Sometimes I am tickled when I ask someone to perform a task such as serve in a certain area of church, and they tell me that they will pray about it and see what God says. That usually tells me that the person does not want to do the job and they need a little time to come up with a good excuse to say no. I don't need to ask God if it is OK for me to do something I have seen him do over and over again.

This is not to say that you should accept every invitation or take on every task. There is the need for wisdom in how we manage our time. But let us not blame God for our unwillingness to do things we know He already wants us to do and we have the time, energy and resources to do.

I don't need to ask God permission to serve in an orphanage or to tutor an at-risk child, when I know I can. When I walk with God, I have an understanding of how I should behave in different situations because I have been listening to Him while walking, and I know His ways.

The reverse of you knowing God's ways is also important – God knows your ways. Yes, God knows everything and He knows our ways, even before our ways become our ways. That is not what is meant here. When we walk with God, our character is developed and He is able to trust us with greater responsibilities – knowing that we can handle them. We become close friends of His and He backs us up because of the developing friendship.

The Bible illustrates such a relationship in the person of Samuel, who was "lent to the Lord, all the days of his life" (1 Samuel 1:28). Samuel remained in the temple. As his relationship with God grew, the Bible tells us that "none of his words fell to the ground" (1 Samuel 3:19).

At first glance, it may seem that this verse

speaks to the accuracy of Samuel's prophecies. It does, but not in the sense that Samuel accurately relayed the things God said. What it is saying is that God "*let* none of his words fall…"

When we walk with God, our character is developed and He is able to trust us with greater responsibilities

In other words, God trusted the relationship that had developed with Samuel so that when Samuel spoke, God said, "Because you have said this I am going to do it." It was a friendship relationship and friends do that for friends – they back each other up.

Prayer

Dear God, I want to be Your friend. I want to walk with You daily, so that I will know Your ways. I want to understand the things You have said in Your word so I may live them out each day. Lord, help me to be ever mindful of the things that please You and the things that don't that I will keep very short accounts with You. Help me to live my life in such a way that You will trust me more. In Jesus name I pray. Amen.

The Enoch Treasure

Nugget 5
TOUCHING OTHERS

So far we have seen some of the tremendous benefits of the *Enoch Treasure*, the friendship with God treasure. There is no relationship trade-off that supersedes being in intimate relationship with God. No wonder the sons of Korah concluded "Better is one day in your courts than a thousand elsewhere" (Psalm 84:10). One wonderful thing about the *Enoch Treasure* is that as you become a closer friend of God, you are not the only beneficiary. This brings us to the fifth nugget of the *Enoch Treasure*:

When you walk with God it affects the people who are around you

Genesis 5 presents 10 generations from Adam. Verse 21 tells us that Enoch was 65 when he had a son by the name of Methuselah (man of the dart). This may seem like just another in the line of descendants, except there is something special about Methuselah – he lived 969 years. Why is that important? It is important because Methuselah lived longer than any human being had ever lived before, or after.

Have you ever stopped to wonder how Methuselah learned the secrets of living longer than any other human being has ever lived? It certainly was not because he was a vegetarian. The Bible does not say much about Methuselah's life, but I imagine that Methuselah enjoyed some good red heifer ribs or kudo stew from time to time. (A kudo

The principles of walking with God work, and they work every time

is an animal somewhat similar to a reindeer, with two long horns. If you have seen a rabbi blow a long shofar, you quite possibly have seen a kudo horn). And to my vegetarian friends – yes, Methuselah probably also enjoyed some falafel, hummus, msabbha, shakshouka, and couscous.

One author wrote about a so-called Methuselah effect – that of living one's life without making any meaningful contribution. That author was oh so wrong. Methuselah teaches us that when a person lives a godly life, it affects not only him or her but it is possible for others to adopt that godly lifestyle and live long and prosper.

Enoch walked with God for 300 years after he fathered Methuselah, and as Enoch walked with God, his offspring learned the secrets of how to live. Does it mean that Methuselah also walked with God? Not necessarily. But what it does show us is that a godly lifestyle is a good lifestyle. Whether or not a person today decides to relentlessly pursue a deep walk with God, the principles of walking with God work, and they work every time.

BIBLICAL PRINCIPLES

There are so many stories of business people who are not Christians, but they have adopted biblical principles in their companies, and have reaped the rich benefits of the God-inspired lifestyle. Parents have followed the principles of childrearing taught in the Bible and as a result, have seen their children grow in the fear and admonition of the Lord. Biblical principles work.

I am not sure why a person would see many biblical principles working in their life and not realize that by making a total commitment to God, they would benefit even more. Perhaps it is because a total commitment requires something of us that we are not willing to give, but as we can see in the case of Enoch, the benefits far outweigh anything else.

If God didn't take Enoch, he could have outlived even his son Methuselah

These days, common buzzwords in leadership circles are "all in," "lean in," or "go long." I encourage you to do this with the *Enoch Treasure* – go all in. Give God your all and allow him to radically transform every aspect of your life. When you do that, those around you may not join you in your walk, but they can't help being challenged by your lifestyle.

I remember soon after I became a Christian that I decided to live a life of commitment to God. Each morning I would wake up and have my devotions. Sometime later, my cousin who was living with us at the time joined in… then my brothers and sisters. Soon my older brother gave his life to the Lord; then my younger brothers and sister did too. Later, one by one, they followed in the waters of baptism.

Living a godly lifestyle is very often contagious, but whether a total commitment is made or not, whether there is tangible change or not, your life speaks of a better way to live. Chances are, if God didn't take Enoch, he could have outlived even his son Methuselah – we will never know.

PASSING ON THE LEGACY

You may have noticed that I have stopped short of saying that there is an automatic transference of godly traits from generation to generation. While walking with God affects those around you, it isn't a guarantee that others will be so affected that they will adopt your lifestyle. Methuselah had a son, Lamech. Enoch's grandson is not to be confused with another Lamech from Genesis 4, who was a descendent of Cain.

Cain's descendant was a self-righteous bigamist who relied on himself and the talents of his sons. Eventually he killed a man for wounding him. Methuselah's son, Lamech on the other hand, had a heart that reflected softness towards the God of his grandfather (remember families were much closer then, and so Lamech would no doubt be influenced by his grandfather Enoch). Later, when Lamech gave birth to a son, he named him saying, "This one will comfort us concerning our work and the toil of our hands, because of the ground which the Lord has cursed."

However, though Lamech (Methuselah's son) had a God consciousness and softness towards God, we know that Lamech later perished alongside other descendants of Methuselah, in the flood that destroyed the world. We can see here that there was a huge difference between the two Lamechs; one was undoubtedly affected by the godly heritage of his grandfather, while the other wasn't.

This may not bring much comfort to a godly father or mother, doing everything to live a righteous life, yet find that some of their children stray. But if Enoch walked with God and lost a few close heirs, perhaps you shouldn't be so hard on yourself. Continue living your life to please God – let Him take care of the rest.

From the timeline of scripture we notice some things – Enoch's son Methuselah died just before the flood. His grandson, Lamech died in the flood at the ripe old age of 777 years old. If you know anything about numbers in the Bible, you know that seven is the number of completion. Though Lamech died in the flood, it seems that God was sending a message to the world – perhaps a promise of completion to His friend Enoch.

Even when all seems lost, don't give up hope. Someone you have been praying for may be going astray, but there is still hope and perhaps when you think things can't get worse, somewhere in the darkest night, a light shines through. Lamech's son, Enoch's great-grandson was that light – his name: Noah.

Prayer

Heavenly Father, I thank You for allowing me to walk with You. I thank you for keeping me, in spite of all those who choose not to come along for the journey. Today I pray for my loved ones. I ask that You will draw them by Your love. Lord, I pray for those who have been hard cases, and I cannot see how they will change. I place them in Your hands and trust You, my friend with those I love so much. Thank You for redeeming them. In Jesus name I pray. Amen.

Nugget 6
DO IT AGAIN

Noah was not yet born when God took Enoch – that happened a few years before his birth. But this was a close family culture, ripe with oral tradition. You will notice from the first few chapters of Genesis that part of a story is told, then it is repeated as more details are added… That was the culture of the day – stories were told and repeated from generation to generation.

I would venture to say that having recently happened, Methuselah would repeat the story of Enoch's life to his children and although they knew the climax of the story, the wide-eyed children would certainly look forward to the part where Methuselah would dramatize how God took Enoch. As Lamech started his family, he also passed down the story of Enoch to his children.

One of his sons, Noah kept hearing this story and developed a great thirst for the type of life Enoch experienced with God. This brings us to our next very important nugget:

The Enoch Treasure may be grasped

Noah was not satisfied with simply hearing about the relationship between his great-grandfather and God. One day Noah said "I want that relationship with God for myself." While the other children may have been contented to hear of Enoch's feats as he walked with God, Noah had a godly jealousy. He was not satisfied with leaving the past in the past – "If it happened for Enoch, it can happen for me," he said. Did it happen for Noah?

After about six months being stuck in Genesis 5, I finally felt the release from God to continue reading through the Bible, and so I turned over to Genesis 6, ready to continue my mission. I didn't get very far before God dropped the next zinger in my lap.

"But Noah found grace in the eyes of the LORD. This is the genealogy of Noah. Noah was a just man, perfect in his generations. **Noah walked with God**" (Genesis 6:8-9).

Bam!!! Here we go again...

I grew up in a home opposite a Salvation Army church. Every time the doors were opened, we were there. Church was a way of life for our family – it was our Sunday school, our entertainment, our picnic, our inspiration, and the list goes on. I don't know how many times I heard the story of Enoch walking with God, but I never ever made the connection that His great-grandson also walked with God. Noah was the second person this was said of in scripture. There are several remarkable features of this, which are relevant to us today.

LESSONS FROM NOAH

First, the *Enoch Treasure* is not a one-time experience. If we get hungry enough, we can also have a close friendship relationship with God, but it must be grasped. There were many who heard the family accounts of the life of Enoch; but Noah grasped it. He also walked with God. As he walked with God, he discovered that God was there all along, seeking to be friends with us. That statement almost sounds blasphemous – That God is seeking our friendship.

In one sense, it seems to put God below man,

If we get hungry enough, we can also have a close friend-ship relation-ship with God, but it must be grasped but it really doesn't. That's because God's grace is scandalous. He seeks out men, women and children who are undeserving (as we all are), plagued by sin with evil in our hearts, and God says: I want you. Come to me and let me wash you and make you holy, so I can pull you close to myself.

Man rebelled against God, and so God personally came in the person of Jesus Christ, God became man, to live among us, in order that He may redeem us unto Himself. This is where Christianity differs from every man-made religion – God makes the sacrifice to restore the relationship with us, so that He may walk with us. Scandalous!

When Jesus came to earth to live among us, He didn't come in a mansion fit for a king, instead his bed was a feed trough. Naturally, as He ministered to others, He himself had others who served Him, but He never allowed this to get to His head, but was the absolute servant leader... He told His disciples "No longer do I call you servants, for a servant does not know what his master is doing; but I have called you friends, for all things that I heard from My Father I have made known to you" (John 15:15).

Then one day, close to His ultimate sacrifice for His friends, he did something even more unimaginable for God to do: He got down on His knees and washed the dirty feet of His disciples...

God kneeling before His friends. This is more grace than words can adequately express. This is a friendship worth grasping.

As Noah heard the stories of his great-grandfather, he discovered a treasure hidden in a field (see Matthew 13:44). He didn't just want to hear the stories about how God took Enoch, he was more interested in the journey Enoch experienced alongside the eternally precious friend. In one sense, you may say **Noah sold all he had, and bought that field with the treasure**.

He pondered the stories in his heart until it became like a fire shut up within his bones, and nothing else would satisfy. And then one day when he could bear it no more something amazing happened – God appeared and said, "Let's take a walk together."

Noah walked with God. Selah.

After this, Noah instinctively knew everything about his life had forever been changed, but he never quite understood how much. Along the journey, he discovered several very important lessons. First, you can walk with God in spite of evil all around you. The earth was so vile and wicked that God decided to destroy it but in the midst of that, Noah stood out like a sore thumb. He stood as an intercessor between God and the complete destruction of man.

Second, when you walk with God his eyes will be upon you. According to Genesis 8:6, "Noah found grace in the eyes of the Lord." It wouldn't be any different – When you are walking with God, His eyes remain on you. When you are having this personal relationship – having your devotions, spending time with Him even in the darkest night, He searches you out like a lover seeks a heartthrob.

You can walk with God in spite of evil all around you

Have you ever felt alone and left out, wondering where God is? Wonder no more. Begin to worship the Lord, let Him know how much you appreciate Him. When you do that you will find that you no longer have to spend time looking for Him.

God's eyes will remain on you and when His eyes are on you, He cannot be very far. Where is God when I am "going through…?" Spend time worshipping Him and He will find you because His eye is on the people who love Him and spend time with Him. When we worship Him in Spirit and truth, the Father seeks us out (John 4:23-24).

The third thing Noah discovered is that when you walk with God, the Lord will tell you His secrets. God decided to destroy the earth but He said I couldn't do it without telling my friend. God will tell you His secrets. He shared His heart with Noah about what He was about to do – friends are like that, they tell each other things… even unimportant things.

When God tells you His secrets, it may not be because He wants you to build an ark. It may not be because He wants you to "read everybody's mail" and reveal things about themselves that no one else knew. It may not even be because He wants you to tell what is about to happen to others.

God will share things with you just because... That's what happens when you become close walking buddies with someone, you share what is on your mind… simple, important, and even funny things.

When God tells you His secrets, it may not be because He wants you to build an ark.

In this case, God gave Noah plans to escape the upcoming destruction. He wanted to protect His friend and so He gave him the blueprints to build the ark. The revelation of God runs really deep, because He is sharing with you and He is the fountain of all knowledge.

Fourth, the Lord will do everything to protect you, His friend. If God didn't give Noah the blueprints to build the ark, Noah would be destroyed too, along with the rest of the world, but God protected His friend. Just as He gave Noah this intricate plan to do something no one else had ever done, it's the same thing with us. God will give us His protective plans to shelter us from coming dangers.

God will give us His protective plans to shelter us from coming dangers

You may not be a doctor, but Dr. God may give you the cure for a disease that would baffle the keenest scientist. You are not an accountant? Don't worry, if God keeps records of the entire earth, surely He can help you to keep records of your finances.

Wondering how you will function in a certain situation, how you are going to get through it? Don't worry, God can in a moment, drop the solution in your lap. Humans function in seconds, and minutes, hours, days, fortnights, months, years, decades, centuries, etc. God functions in moments… and in a moment, in the twinkling of an eye, you can be changed from failure to success.

There have been many great world inventions and perhaps you may be wondering if all the great inventions have already been made. People have been creating music for centuries, yet there are still new sounds, new tunes, new music; let God show you His precise plans, plans for things the world does not even know it needs.

When God gave Noah the blueprints for the ark, the world did not know it needed an ark. In fact, the world didn't even know what an ark was. God may give you the idea for a *jugadoo* or a *binkish*... What are they? I don't know, they haven't been invented as yet.

When Noah dared to walk on the wild side with God, he didn't do it because he needed an ark; he did it because he desired to walk with the One who desired to walk with him more. When he responded to the call of the Lord to walk with Him, God in turn gave Noah creative ideas, for things unseen.

"Call unto me, and I will answer you, and show you great and mighty things which you do not know" (Jeremiah 33:3).

When God gave Noah the blueprints for the ark, the world did not know it needed an ark.

Fifth, Noah like Enoch before him, discovered that when you walk with God even your kin is covered. The heavenly Father took Noah, his wife and children into the ark.

Many of us are praying for family members – spouses, brothers, cousins, etc. God wants to save your family. He will show you ways you can reach them, and as you pray for them God works on their hearts, wooing them to Him. Of course, they still have free will to accept Him or not, but you can be sure that God is working in an extra special way to draw your kin to Himself.

Finally, Noah discovered that walking with God is a walk of obedience. There is a saying, "liberty comes through carelessness." Sometimes when you walk with a friend they start to treat you as if they no longer hold you in high regard. Noah however recognized that in spite of the fact that he was now "walking buddies" with God, respect was still due to the Lord. When God told Him to build an ark, Noah built an ark. He did not question God; he just did it.

I heard a very good example of how it is possible to be a good friend, yet still maintain the respect that is due. One of the presidents of the United States enjoys a good game of basketball. He often invites friends he had before he became president to shoot hoops with him at the White House. An interviewer asked the friends if they allowed him to win sometimes and the answer was "absolutely not." They played against him as hard as they ever did, not giving him an inch on the court. However, at the end of the day, those friends still call him Mr. President.

When we walk with God, we must respect Him. He is still holy, righteous and awesome in every way. When we walk with God, we walk with someone infinitely bigger than us. We become friends, but we never lose the respect and honor due to Him.

Noah however recognized that in spite of the fact that he was now "walking buddies" with God, respect was still due to the Lord.

When God told Noah to build an ark, Noah must have asked Him, "What's an ark?" Yet he was obedient. He built the ark. If a relationship with God is important enough to be grasped, it is important enough for us to keep holding onto, even after we are drawn closer into God's presence.

Prayer

Dear Heavenly Father, I come thirsty. I am no longer satisfied with simply living the Christian life. I want a closer walk with You. I must have this relationship with You, because I have fallen in love with You. Thank You for the great sacrifice You made to have a relationship with me. I can never repay You, but I give you my all. Touch me and fill me with Your Holy Spirit... truly be my friend indeed. Come Holy Spirit. Amen.

Nugget 7
WALKING DIFFERENTLY

One often-overlooked fact relating to Enoch walking with God is the environment in which Enoch lived. Long before Enoch was born, Earth had experienced its first murder. Adam's son Cain, killed his brother Abel, out of jealousy, because God was pleased with Abel's sacrifice, while he rejected Cain's.

Cain's action caused him to be cursed, the ground no longer being fertile for him, regardless of how hard he worked farming. Cain pleaded with God for mercy and God placed a mark upon him, effectively saving him from further vengeance. As Cain went east of Eden and had descendants, his murderous DNA continued to bear fruit. Evil reigned.

It wasn't until many years later, that Adam & Eve had a grandson, Enosh, that men turned their hearts back to God (Genesis 4:26). However, there is no sign that this turning back to God bore much fruit. Sin continued to reign and it was in this environment that Enoch was born. Enoch therefore had to make a choice to be different. This brings us to the next nugget:

You cannot walk with God and live like everyone else

From one of our earlier nuggets, we know that living is different from walking with God. Enoch therefore had to make a choice – a concerted effort to reject the culture of the day, to not simply live. Everyone else was doing his/her own thing. Then came a sliver of hope when Enosh turned his heart to God. (Enosh is not to be confused with Enoch who came much later).

How awful it must have been living at a time when no one paid any attention to God. What could have been that catalyst that forced Enosh to decide that things could not continue that way anymore and caused him to turn his heart to God? Why was it that no one succeeded in shifting the course of history?

No one, that is, until Enoch. The Bible is silent as to exactly what made Enoch different from everyone else before him. What we do know is that God never stopped wanting to restore the relationship between people and Himself.

In Genesis 1, He created man in His own image. In Genesis 2, God breathed his very breath into man. In Genesis 3, Adam and Eve sinned, but God is quick to point out that one day He would send a seed who would bruise the head of the Devil – the seed, Jesus Christ Himself. In Genesis 4 as things continued to deteriorate, Enosh is born and a few turned their hearts back to God, but this wasn't enough. It wasn't the relationship God wanted.

There is only one common denominator in all scripture leading up to this point – God. He was working in the hearts of people everywhere, calling them back to Himself, making a way for the relationship to be restored.

Finally, He found someone who heard the call, someone who dared to be different. When Enoch heard the call, he discovered the missing treasure in his life and the life of everyone else – that God was always there... wanting to walk with him.

Enoch therefore had to make a choice – a concerted effort to reject the culture of the day

When Enoch decided to

walk with God he discovered something – the road walking with God is a lonely one, but it didn't matter; one person plus God is a majority every time. One person walking with God can change the course of history. One person walking with God changes all the rules.

Later, hearing the stories of His great-grandfather, Noah grasped at the supernatural and he discovered the same thing Enoch recognized earlier – God wants to walk with us, more than we want to walk with Him. Elijah, the prophet later discovered the same thing – God is ready to walk with us, even before we are ready to walk with Him.

Throughout history, men, women and children have stumbled upon this treasure – and they have walked with God. Today, you are reading a little book called *The Enoch Treasure*. No doubt you have read other books before, but you didn't come across this book by accident. Perhaps a friend told you about it, you may have seen an advertisement in a magazine or online or it may have been a gift. Regardless of how this book came to be in your hands, God led you to it.

Now there is a decision to be made: Will you

continue to merely live, or will you walk with God? I can tell you right now, the majority of the world isn't walking with God. And so, if you decide to take this path, you will find that you have to live differently from everyone else.

What is optional for some will not be optional for you. What are some of these things? Don't worry; when you walk with God, you will instinctively know the things that are displeasing to Him.

The call to walk with God is not the same as the call of Jesus in Matthew 7:13—"Enter by the narrow gate; for wide *is* the gate and broad *is* the way that leads to destruction, and there are many who go in by it."

You see…there are many Christians who have already chosen the narrow gate that leads to life – yet they are not walking with God. The walk with God is a walk off the beaten narrow path.

Noah grasped at the supernatural and he discovered the same thing Enoch recognized earlier – God wants to walk with us, more than we want to walk with Him

This is a little book with a lot of salt. Salt makes you thirsty and I pray this book has helped to make you thirsty for a relationship that will change your life as well as everyone else around you.

I don't know what will be your adventure; I can't predict what you will encounter along the way. All I can promise you is that there is an unquantifiable component, a friendship factor that will become a part of your experience…that eyes have not seen nor ears heard, what God has in store for you.

Now it is time for your prayer…

Prayer

Points to Ponder

Nugget 1– More than Living

1. Name a few persons you know who you think are walking with God.

_____

_____

_____

2. What are some of the characteristics that you admire about these persons?

_____

_____

_____

3. What can you adopt from their lifestyle that will help you in your personal walk with God?

_____

_____

_____

4. As you examine your own life, what are some of the things you do, that others could notice to indicate that you are walking with God?

_____

_____

_____

_____

_____

5. When you think of being created in God's image, with the DNA of His breath flowing through you, who do you see when you look in the mirror? What are some of the things preventing you from being more like Him?

_____

_____

_____

_____

_____

_____

_____

Nugget 2 – The Regular Life

1. List some of your daily actions that distract from a close friendship relationship with God?

_____

_____

_____

2. How difficult is it for you to live a regular life and walk with God?

_____

_____

_____

3. Many people in a general manner know that they are special to God. However, on a personal level, do you really feel like you are special to God? How so?

_____

_____

_____

4. When it comes to their sexual life, many people separate it from their relationship with God. Why do you believe it is so difficult to manage this aspect of our lives and maintain a close relationship with God?

_____

_____

_____

5. Do you feel inhibited before God when it comes to your sexual life? Why or why not?

_____

_____

_____

6. Infidelity seems to get many people into trouble. If you are in a relationship, how can you ensure that you remain faithful to your partner? If single, how do you maintain/sustain purity before God?

_____

_____

_____

_____

Nugget 3 – Beyond Death

1. Describe your ideas or feelings about heaven.

_____

_____

_____

2. What do you imagine when you think about heaven? Have you had heavenly experiences? Explain.

_____

_____

_____

3. How cool would it be to go to heaven and come back to earth? What are some things you think you would want to do there before returning?

_____

_____

_____

4. In the Lord's Prayer, Jesus taught "Your Kingdom Come, Your will be done on earth as it is in heaven..." What are some of the heavenly blessings you'd like to come to earth?

_____

_____

_____

5. Describe the time in your life when you were most deeply touched/affected by your relationship with God.

_____

_____

_____

6. We pose a radical thought – Can we become such good friends of God that He will feel that He is denying Himself if He does not come to be with us? What are some of the things you can do that would cause God to want to walk with you?

_____

_____

_____

_____

Nugget 4 – Walk and Learn

1. What do you believe are some other benefits of walking with God?

_____

_____

_____

2. Highlight examples from your life and the Bible that show that God indeed wants to walk with you.

_____

_____

_____

3. What are some obstacles/hurdles in your personal life that would make the commitment to walk with God challenging for you, family, friends, work, etc?

_____

_____

_____

_____

4. Enoch was not sinless, after all he was human. But he knew God was holy and so he needed to keep short accounts with Him, meaning Enoch did not wait very long to make things right. Is this your approach? What are some of the factors that keep us from making it right with God quickly?

_____

_____

_____

_____

_____

Nugget 5 –Touching Others

1. When you think about walking with God, who are the people in your life right now who you think would benefit from your commitment?

_____

_____

_____

_____

_____

2. Are there others close to you who have not adopted a godly lifestyle, but show tenderness toward God? Commit to pray for them regularly.

_____

_____

_____

_____

3. What biblical principles can you adopt in your occupation, which would bring you and others around you long lasting success?

_____

_____

_____

4. Apart from praying for others close to you, what are some practical things you can do to encourage family and friends to have a closer relationship with God?

_____

_____

_____

_____

5. What is the legacy that you think you will leave to your family and friends, if you take this life-changing step of walking with God?

_____

_____

_____

Nugget 6 –Do It Again

1. What does it mean to you that the *Enoch Treasure* must be grasped? How radical would you say is your approach to wanting to have a close friendship with God?

_____

_____

_____

2. Which of the five lessons that Noah learned as he walked with God means the most to you? Why?

_____

_____

_____

3. What aspects of your life are you embarrassed to make God a part of or think He's not concerned with… social, physical, mental, financial… etc?

_____

_____

_____

4. God gave Noah blueprints to build an ark, when the world didn't even know it needed one. Are there ideas/plans God has given you that you may be sitting on? If so, what are some of the reasons you haven't acted on these?

_____

_____

_____

5. Many people have gotten close to God, only to fall into the sin of pride or becoming too familiar with the things of God. What are some of the other challenges people face in getting very close to God?

_____

_____

_____

_____

Nugget 7—Walking Differently

1. Enoch had to make a choice to walk with God. You would have to do the same to step out on this journey. List the things that you think would prevent you from making the choice right now.

_____

_____

_____

_____

2. What are some areas you believe you need to change in your life in order to have a closer walk with God?

_____

_____

_____

3. Are there relationships or friendships that you may have to sever in order to have a closer walk with God?

_____

_____

_____

4. Are there good things you do right now, that you may have to give up in order to have a closer walk with God?

_____

_____

_____

_____

_____

5. What are some of the first steps you need to take on your journey with God?

_____

_____

_____

_____

_____

_____

_____

Study Guide

General Questions

1. Which nugget speaks to where you are in your spiritual life right now?

2. Which nugget do you identify with most and would easily grasp?

3. Compared to the culture of Enoch's time, do you think the impact of your culture today makes it more difficult for you to walk with God?

4. Do you feel so close to God that you share everything with him... even funny things? Go ahead, He wants to hear them.

5. Name a few people who you think would benefit from reading *The Enoch Treasure*? Go ahead and tell them about it.

Group Icebreaker Questions

Nugget 1—More Than Living

1. Do you have a best friend? What makes him or her such a special friend to you?

2. What is your favorite attribute of God? On a scale of 1-10, rate your top 5 attributes of God.

Nugget 2—The Regular Life

1. What occupations do you think make it more challenging to walk with God? Why do you say this?

2. Who is your favorite musical celebrity? Why? What are some of the songs you think will last a lifetime?

Nugget 3—Beyond Death

1. What is the first thing you would want to ask God, when you see Him?

2. What is your favorite song about heaven?

Nugget 4—Walk and Learn

1. Who have you been friends with for the longest time? For how long have you been friends and why do you think this friendship has lasted so long?

2. What do you like to do most with friends when you get together?

Nugget 5—Touching Others

1. How long would you like to live to be? Why?

2. What family traditions have you adopted from your parents that you continue now, or plan to continue in the future?

Nugget 6—Do It Again

1. If you could re-live your childhood, what memory would you like to experience again?

2. If you could go back in time to Bible days, is there a particular time you would like to experience?

Nugget 7—Walking Differently

1. How many friends from your childhood do you still have?

2. Have you ever had to do a friend purge or social media purge?

3. If you find that things in your life are getting stale, how do you make changes to re-invigorate your life?

Additional Resources

One of the greatest tragedies of the Christian church today is that it worships a God it does not really know. **"Worship 101: Discovering the God We Worship in 101 Ways"** seeks to help us understand who God is. The book presents a combination of 101 names, attributes and characteristics of God directly from the Bible (with supporting verses) which may be used to enhance our worship experience.

This book is punctuated by several sections of down to earth practical suggestions aimed at moving our worship experience from the superficial to one based on real knowledge, increased reverence and intimacy with God. One of the beautiful qualities of Worship 101 is its universal appeal for Christians of all denominations. Because the major emphasis is on scripture, rather than personal opinions, the book will be attractive to a wide range of believers from the traditional/conservative to the modern/liberal. This book is one that will be valuable to young Christians and inspiring to older ones.

COMING SOON

Holy Friend: Walking With the Holy Spirit.

In his upcoming book, Dr. Cunningham takes a look at the person and work of the Paraclete, the One Who Comes Alongside Us, the Holy Spirit. Continuing on the theme of "Friendship With God," this book takes us on a personal journey of learning who the Holy Spirit is, His fruit, giftings, callings and how He empowers the Christian for service. This book is for anyone who desires to learn more about the third person of the Godhead.

To invite Dr. Chris Cunningham to speak at your conference or ministry, please contact him through his church's ministry website: www.GOChurchVA.com

Sample topics: * The Enoch Treasure * Worship * Evangelism * Growing in the Supernatural * Normal Supernatural Christianity * Travailing Prayers and the Heart Cry of the Spirit * Prayer and Intercession * Perseverance in Prayer *

Leadership Training:
* How to Develop an Effective Prayer Ministry
* Altar Ministry that Breaks the Chain
*Anatomy of Planning an Event.

Made in the USA
Middletown, DE
08 June 2019